Parenting From
Your Heart

Sharing the Gifts of Compassion,
Connection, and Choice

*A Presentation of Nonviolent
Communication™ ideas and their use by*

Inbal Kashtan

PuddleDancer
P R E S S

2240 Encinitas Blvd., Ste. D-911, Encinitas, CA 92024
email@PuddleDancer.com • www.PuddleDancer.com

For additional information:
Center for Nonviolent Communication
5600 San Francisco Rd., NE, Suite A, Albuquerque, NM 87109
Ph: 505-244-4041 • Fax: 505-247-0414 • Email: cnvc@cnvc.org • Website: www.cnvc.org

ISBN: 978-1-892005-08-3

Contents

Parenting From Your Heart

Introduction

How can we deal with our two-year-old when she grabs her friend's toys? What might we say to a four-year-old who refuses to let other children slide on the playground? How can we talk with a teenager about the chores he has left undone—again? How do we protect our children when their choices endanger their safety? What resources will help us work with our own anger, frustration, or pain when communication with our children seems strained or non-existent?

As parents, we are constantly faced with situations like these. Multiply the children and the challenges mount. Add the pressures of work (or unemployment), money (or lack thereof), time, relationships, and other commitments, and the pot threatens to boil over. Then, for some, there are the stresses of raising children alone, without a partner, extended family, or community. And there are myriad additional challenges many parents face. It is no wonder parents yearn for support, guidance, and relief. Yet when we turn to parenting books or experts, the advice we find is often contradictory and may not align with our own values and hopes for our children and families. Even when we do find an idea we want to try, changing habits and patterns in relationships can be enormously challenging in itself.

In this booklet, I present to parents and others who are connected with children a brief introduction to how Nonviolent

Communication™ (NVC) may support their parenting in practical, immediate ways. I particularly hope to address parents' yearning for deeper connection with themselves, their partners, and their children, and their desire to contribute, through parenting, to fostering peace in the world. The approach I describe, as you will see, goes beyond immediate solutions and into the realm of personal and social transformation.

This booklet explores a variety of topics and situations and offers ten exercises to help you put into practice what you are learning as you shift or adapt your parenting approaches. However, it is by no means a comprehensive exploration of NVC and parenting. I have not touched upon many topics that have come up in my workshops and classes, on the NVC-parenting email list, and in my own life. I hope, nonetheless, that what I have covered here will be practical enough to offer you some concrete tools for deepening connection with your children, and exciting enough to encourage you to consider learning even more. If you choose to put these ideas into practice and they make a difference in your family life, I would love to hear from you.

For a review of the basic steps of NVC and additional information on NVC, see the back of the booklet.

"Power-over" versus "Power-with"

When parents want children to do something their children don't want to do, it's often tempting to force the children's compliance by using the enormous physical, emotional, and practical power adults have over them (by practical, I mean that adults have much greater access to society's resources and control over the course of their own—and their children's—lives). Yet I am convinced that attempting to coerce a child to do something she or he doesn't want to do neither works effectively in the short term nor supports families' long-term needs. (The only exception comes when there is threat to health or safety, in which case NVC suggests that we use non-punitive, protective force.) In NVC, we refer to using power to enforce what we want as "power-over," in contrast with using power to meet everyone needs, which we refer to as "power-with."

Maria, a parent who had read some of my articles, asked me a question that points directly to the temptation to use the control we have over resources to influence a child's behavior (note that all people's names have been changed):

I've been "bargaining" with my two-year-old son Noel using rewards and consequences, and sometimes it seems to me that it's quite effective. At least, it gets him to do what I want, such as eat the food on his plate. Yet I'm somehow uncomfortable with this. Is there a problem with rewards and consequences if they work?

I do think that there is a problem with rewards and consequences, because in the long run, they rarely work in the ways we hope. In fact, I think that they are likely to backfire. Marshall Rosenberg explores this point by asking parents two questions: "What do you want your child to do?" and "What do you want your child's reasons to be for doing so?" Parents rarely want their children to do something out of fear of consequences, guilt, shame, obligation, or even a desire for reward.

In this context, when I hear parents—or parenting experts—say that consequences are effective, I often wonder what they mean. I believe "effective" usually means that parents get compliance from children—that children do what parents tell them to do—at least for a while. Both the goal (compliance) and the means (rewards and consequences) come at a price. They not only involve fear, guilt, shame, obligation, or desire for reward, they are also often accompanied by anger or resentment. And because rewards and consequences are *extrinsic* motivations, children become dependent on them and lose touch with their *intrinsic* motivation to meet their own and others' needs.

I believe that the most powerful and joyful *intrinsic* motivation human beings have for taking any action is the desire to meet our own and others' needs. Both children and adults act out of this intrinsic motivation when they feel genuinely connected to themselves and each other, when they trust that their needs matter to the other, and when they experience the freedom to *choose* to contribute to the other.

If we want our children to experience intrinsic motivation for doing what we ask them to do, we can shift our focus away from authority and imposed discipline and toward paying as much attention as possible to everyone's long-term needs. This may take more time in the moment because it means going beyond the present problem and remembering what matters most in the big picture. Yet the time is worth the investment. In the long run, families can experience deeper connection, trust, and harmony, and children can learn powerful life skills. I believe that most parents find these goals much more appealing and exciting than mere compliance.

Instead of rewards and consequences, NVC offers three starting places for connecting with others: offering empathy, expressing one's own observations, feelings, needs and requests, and connecting with oneself through self-empathy. In the next three sections, I will explore each of these options in relation to the question Maria asked me.

Empathy for a Child

Empathizing with another person opens the door to deep understanding and connection. When Maria approaches Noel, she can begin with the premise that some of his needs are not being met. Even with a toddler or a child not used to NVC language, a parent is likely to be able to ferret out his needs.

When Noel pushes his food away or says "no," Maria can try to understand how he feels and the needs he is trying to meet instead of trying to change his actions. She can ask herself silently: Is he saying no to the food because he's trying to meet his need for pleasure—does he dislike the food? Is he distracted by other things and so wants to meet a need to focus on what's interesting to him? Is he annoyed because he needs autonomy— to choose what and when to eat? Perhaps he is not hungry, and so feels confused because he needs trust in his ability to recognize his own body's cues?

Having connected mentally with her son's needs, Maria may consider checking her understanding with him to see if any of these guesses fit. She may ask, for example: "Are you frustrated because you want food you enjoy more?" "Are you distracted? You want to pay attention to your game?" "Are you annoyed because *you* want to choose when to eat?" The language can be simplified if the parent is concerned that the child might not understand. But it is important to keep in mind that toddlers understand more than they can verbalize. Furthermore, by including feelings and needs in their vocabulary, parents are teaching children emotional literacy. Even if the child doesn't reply, many parents will notice that their own tone of voice and body language have changed simply because they have connected with the child's needs—and that a potential power struggle has been defused. Now Maria can move on to seek strategies that could meet both people's needs.

In giving empathy, I encourage people to let go of the specific aim of getting their children to do what they want in the specific way they want it done, and instead, to focus on connecting with their children. At the same time, it is equally important for parents to stay in touch with their own underlying needs. Maria may consider what, if anything, she'd be willing to do differently to increase the likelihood of meeting her son's needs without giving up on her needs. Integrating her child's needs into her strategies could include changing the daily menu, offering food somewhere in the house where her son can eat as he plays, creating and eating playful, colorful food together, and many more. The strategy doesn't matter as much as being attuned to both her own and her child's needs. In this way, by attending to her child's underlying needs, she would also be attending to her own. There is ultimately no conflict between their needs—they just have different strategies and priorities at that moment.

Sharing One's Own Experience

In using NVC, creating a quality of connection that enables everyone to have their needs met is the priority. Sometimes this means empathizing with the child's needs, but other times it means paying close attention to how parents express themselves. When they pause to reflect on what they have been communicating, parents frequently discover that they have been repeating what they want their child to do ("I said, stop playing and eat your food!"), but their child often tunes them out. Instead, parents can express their full experience in that moment: what they are responding to (an observation), their feelings, their needs, and then what they would like from the child. Most people—children included—are more open to considering one another when they understand each other's underlying feelings and needs, because they connect with the human being behind the request.

When Noel won't eat, Maria might say, "When I see you pushing the food on the table and not putting it in your mouth, I'm worried because I'd like to help your body be strong and healthy. Would you be willing to eat what's on your plate?" The catch here is, since most human beings have a huge need for autonomy—especially when we fear our need for autonomy won't be met—it's possible that her son will say no! This is precisely the reason that I wouldn't want to force him. I believe that the more children hear demands, the less they want to do what parents ask of them. The result is that both parents and children miss the joy of cooperation and mutual consideration. Therefore, how Maria responds to the "no" is pivotal to nurturing Noel's trust in her willingness to embrace both her needs *and* his. She may choose to empathize with her son, or she may choose to express her own feelings and needs again. This time she might say, "I feel frustrated because I need more ease and cooperation around meal times," or "I'm confused. I'd like to understand what you want to do."

Each expression in NVC ends with a request that usually begins, "Would you be willing to . . .?" Asking for a reply maintains the flow of dialogue about a problem. Yet often I find that parents repeat the same request, which tells me that they are still very intent on getting the child to do exactly what they want her or him to do. The child often senses that and objects even more strenuously. So another helpful focus for dealing with "no" is to pay attention to the *kinds* of requests parents make. Maria can take notice of what she is saying once again: Is she repeating the request to eat? If so, then it is likely that Noel hears this as a demand. She can then try to consider other strategies for meeting her needs and ask for that. For example, she might ask Noel if he'd be willing to tell her *when* he'd like to eat. He might say five minutes. Then she can set a timer, and in five minutes he has met his need for choice and will likely sit down to eat in good spirits.

Self-Empathy

Self-empathy in NVC means checking in with your own feelings and needs. This may seem odd at first, but I and many other NVC practitioners have found it profoundly effective for increasing self-acceptance, self-connection, and inner peace. Just taking a minute before reacting can reduce anger and prevent a power struggle!

If Maria chooses to start with self-empathy, her inner dialogue may sound something like this: "Wow, I'm feeling so stressed out! I want to rest. Plus I'm worried because I need confidence that Noel is getting the nutrition his body needs. And I'm so frustrated because I'd like cooperation around caring for his health. I'm also troubled because I need to understand what's going on for him—I really have no idea!" It may take Maria some time to recognize her feelings and needs but with practice, she will learn to connect with herself more easily.

Having gotten clearer about her needs, Maria can now consider what she would like to do. Each of her needs might be fulfilled through a variety of different strategies. Would she want to empathize with Noel to try to understand what's going on for him? Express her feelings, needs and requests to him? Consult with Noel's physician about whether to worry about how much he's eating? Talk with her partner or friends about it? Read a book about toddlers and eating? Give Noel more choice about what to eat? Play together with his food? Again, strategies that come from understanding her needs are more likely to meet those needs.

I don't know anyone who was brought up practicing self-empathy. The novelty of self-empathy, combined with the effort it takes to make time for it, can make it seem like an impossible luxury. Yet self-empathy can give us "breathing room" for facing life, much like a meditation practice. While it may not solve every problem, it may actually help us accept the times when we cannot find a "fix." Through self-empathy, we can provide for ourselves some very powerful resources: connection and nurturing for ourselves; focus on what matters most to us; access to creative problem-solving; space to grow and deepen our skills as parents; confidence that we will act more often in ways that bring us joy and satisfaction; and the sweetest thing of all: trust and connection with our loved ones.

Why Take the Time for Connection?

The ways parents interact with their children contribute to shaping children's understanding of themselves, their parents, human nature, and the world around them. A parent who takes a toy away from a toddler who had just taken it from another child, while saying, "No grabbing," teaches both children that grabbing is okay—for those with more power. A parent who unilaterally imposes a curfew implies that a teenager can't be trusted to make thoughtful decisions about his life. Instead, in both words and actions, parents can convey two key ideas: (1) Everyone's needs matter, and (2) If we connect sufficiently we can find strategies that will work for everyone.

By hearing the feelings and needs beneath our children's words and behaviors, we can offer them precious gifts. We can help them understand, express, and find ways to meet their needs; model for them the capacity to empathize with others; give them a vision of a world where everyone's needs matter; and help them see that many of the desires that human beings cling to—having the room clean, right now!, watching television, making money—are really strategies for meeting deeper needs. Children can learn that by taking time to discover their deeper needs, they are more likely to devise strategies that are truly likely to meet those needs.

There is a further blessing when we allow ourselves to be affected by our children's feelings and needs: we can find strategies to meet our needs that are not at a cost to our children. This eases a great deal of pain many of us experience when we think that we must accept strategies that work only for us but not for our children.

Lastly, by sharing our inner world of feelings and needs with our children, we give them opportunities all too rare in our society: to know their parents well, to discover the effects of their actions without being blamed for them, and to experience the power and joy of contributing to meeting others' needs.

EXERCISE 1
Basic Translations

Key Ideas:

- **Observations:** Description of what is seen or heard without added interpretations or judgments. For example, instead of "She's having a temper tantrum," you could say, "She is lying on the floor crying and kicking." If referring to what someone said, quote as much as possible instead of rephrasing.

- **Feelings:** Your emotions rather than your thoughts or interpretations about what others are doing. For example, instead of "I feel manipulated," which includes an interpretation of another's behavior, you could say, "I feel uncomfortable." Avoid the following phrasing: "I feel like . . ." and "I feel that . . ."–the next words will be thoughts, not feelings.

- **Needs:** Feelings are caused by needs, which are universal and ongoing and not dependent on the actions of particular individuals. State your need rather than the other person's actions as the cause. For example, "I feel annoyed *because I* need support" rather than "I feel annoyed *because you* didn't do the dishes."

- **Requests:** Concrete, immediate, and stated in positive action language (what you want instead of what you don't want). For example, "Would you be willing to come back tonight at the time we've agreed?" rather than "Would you make sure not to be late again?" By definition, making requests implies that we are willing to hear a "no," and view it as an opportunity for further dialogue.

- **Empathy:** In NVC, we empathize with others by guessing their feelings and needs. Instead of trying to "get it right," we aim to understand. The observation and request are sometimes dropped.

Using the feelings and needs lists found at the back of this booklet and your own understanding, write some guesses about what the parents' and children's feelings and needs might be in the following scenarios.

1. Parent to child:

    a. Parent says to child: "Clean up your room NOW!"

    What might be the parent's feelings? _____

    What might be the parent's needs? _____

    b. Parent says to child: "Why aren't you listening to me?"

    What might be the parent's feelings? _____

    What might be the parent's needs? _____

    c. Parent says to child: "That's a rude thing to say."

    What might be the parent's feelings? _____

    What might be the parent's needs? _____

2. Child to parent:

    a. Child says to parent: "No, I will NOT clean my room!"

    What might be the child's feelings? _____

    What might be the child's needs? _____

    b. Child says to parent: "You just don't care about me!"

    What might be the child's feelings? _____

    What might be the child's needs? _____

    c. Child says to parent: "I don't want to talk about it."

    What might be the child's feelings? _____

    What might be the child's needs? _____

EXERCISE 2
Translating into NVC

Write down something you've said to your child that you would like to try saying using NVC. Translate the statement into observations, feelings, needs, and requests. (The request doesn't have to "solve the problem"—it's just the beginning of a dialogue!)

Example:

Original statement: "No hitting! Go to your room right now!"

NVC statement: "When I see you hit Max and see Max crying, I feel sad because I need safety for everyone. Would you be willing to tell me what was going on?"

Your Original statement: _____ .

When I see/hear _____ .

I feel _____ .

Because I need _____ .

Would you be willing to _____ ?

Compare your responses with some of the examples I've given in the previous sections.

Beyond Power Struggles

Tantrums and power struggles are the bane of many parents' existence. Yet at the root of every tantrum and power struggle are unmet needs. When one person chooses to step out of the power struggle, communication can begin and harmony can be restored. Consider the following scenario.

Four-year-old Alyssa stands at the top of a slide telling the two other children waiting behind her on the play structure to go away. The other children don't seem very happy about the situation. After gently trying to coax her to come down, her father, Dave, states, "Alyssa, you have to let other children play or we're going home." Hearing this, Alyssa yells back, "No! I don't want to go home!" And she remains at the top of the slide. The children and their parents are looking. Now Dave starts to get really mad. "Come down this minute Alyssa," he calls back. "I will NOT," responds his daughter.

What will happen next? Dave may ask again or threaten to leave the park if she doesn't come down immediately. Alyssa may or may not comply. If she does not comply, Dave may or may not enforce the consequence. If Dave tries to physically remove her, she may become rigid, or kick and scream, making it nearly impossible to move her. Meanwhile Alyssa's little brother, who had been playing happily in the sand, begins crying because *he* didn't do anything wrong and *he* doesn't want to leave the park! A fun outing ends in a power struggle and spoiled moods for everyone.

Moving Between Self-Empathy, Empathy, and Expression

How might this situation play out in NVC? Having heard Alyssa tell other children to stay away, Dave might notice first his inner reaction. He might decide to take a moment for self-empathy: "Everyone's looking! I'm feeling embarrassed. I want acceptance from other parents. I'm also frustrated because I want our time together to flow more easily." Not only is Dave focused on his needs instead of reacting, this self-empathy moment might remind him that reacting angrily usually doesn't work out for him! Having taken this breath, Dave may notice that he wants to connect with Alyssa, and he may decide to guess what might be going on for her.

Dave: Hey Alyssa, are you enjoying the slide? Are you telling the children to stay away because you want some space to play? *(Instead of judging Alyssa's words to the other children as inappropriate or telling her to stop, Dave guesses that it may come out of Alyssa's need for space.)*

Alyssa: Yup! It's fun to be up here by myself!

Dave: So you're enjoying yourself. You like being independent up there.

Alyssa (swinging on the bar above the slide seat): Wheeeeee!

Dave has not said anything about what he would like, but he has taken the first step to connecting with Alyssa. By empathizing with her feelings and needs, he demonstrated to her that he understands her actions without judgment or blame. From here he has more chance of being heard.

Dave: I'm noticing the other children are not having so much fun, so I'm worried. I'd like everyone to be able to have fun at the park. Would you be willing to slide down now so everyone can get a turn?

Some children might agree now, but Alyssa refuses.

Dave: Are you pretty frustrated because *you* want to choose how to play? *(Instead of hearing Alyssa's "no" as a challenge to his authority Dave tries to understand the feelings and needs that led her to say "no.")*

Alyssa: Yes! Yes! Yes! I'm not coming down!

Dave: Alyssa, I want you to be able to make your own decisions. I'm also frustrated and want consideration for everyone here. Do you have any ideas about how you can have fun and make decisions and other children can enjoy themselves, too? *(By including his commitment to meeting Alyssa's needs along with his desire to attend to the other children's needs, Dave avoids a perception—and sometimes a reality—that only one side of the issue matters to him. A commitment to both sides' needs is crucial if we want to find solutions that truly work for all.)*

Alyssa: They can go play on the other slide.

Dave: I'm glad you're considering options. Why don't you check with them to see if that will work for them? *(Even though this is not an option Dave prefers, he considers it. For Alyssa to be willing to consider other options, she needs to trust that Dave would consider other options, too. This is a crucial moment. If Dave is intent on one course of action, it's likely to trigger resistance on Alyssa's part.)*

Alyssa to the two children: Would you play on the other slide?

One child: No!

Second child: It's not as much fun as this one. I want to slide on *this* one.

Dave: So, sweetheart, it looks like they still want to play on this slide, and I'd really like to respect what they would enjoy, too. So, any other ideas, or would you be willing to slide down now and give them a turn?

Many children, if they trust that they will not be coerced, would be willing to work things out by now. But some children have a harder time. Imagine Alyssa saying, "I don't care what they want, I'm not coming down." Even the most patient parent would likely "lose it" by now. How much patience can we expect from ourselves in the face of a very determined young child? Yet the alternative is not so appealing, either—a tantrum, a power struggle, regret about how we spoke to our child. So Dave might try self-empathy again, to give himself a little more space to choose how to act.

In situations like this, anger is often the emotion that surfaces most easily. Dave might therefore begin by expressing his anger internally: "Urggg! I'm soooo angry! Why can't she just be reasonable?!" However, Dave wouldn't stop here, because anger keeps us focused on what we *don't* like instead of helping us connect with our needs and what constructive thing we *would* like. Connecting with his feelings and needs underneath the anger, Dave might continue: "I'm really disappointed. I want to have fun and to connect with my daughter." With self-empathy, Dave shifted from anger to acknowledging his own needs for fun and connection.

Creative Strategies Arise Out of Connection

As long as Dave simply demanded that his daughter get off the slide, the situation was unlikely to meet either of their needs—hers for autonomy, his for connection, and both of theirs for play. (Play is both a need and a powerful strategy for moving through stressful situations with children. Many chores and conflicts can be turned into play—a transformation that can create greater harmony between parents and children.) With self-connection and an empathic connection with his daughter, it will be much easier for him now to arrive at a creative strategy to meet both their needs.

Dave (in a playful tone): So you like being so high up and making decisions? *(Dave connects again with his daughter's needs.)*

Alyssa: Yeah!

Dave (smiling): How do I get up there with you? Should I walk up the slide or take the ladder? *(Dave finds a strategy that meets his daughter's need to make decisions and his need for connection.)*

Alyssa: You can't come up here, it's just for kids!

Dave: Well, I want to play with you, and since you don't seem to be coming down, I guess I'll figure out how to get up there. *(Dave stays playful as a strategy for connection. His daughter is not in a power struggle as long as he is not.)*

Alyssa: Walk up the slide!

Dave pretends to try and fail. His daughter and the other children laugh. They all proceed to play and the tension passes.

At what point would I suggest stopping the dialogue and trying a different course of action? I would move more quickly when there is a question of safety or when taking more time for dialogue seriously impairs other people's ability to meet their needs. Dave can track the other children: Are they playing and having fun, or are some upset because their own needs for play aren't met? Are they watching, and if so, are they curious about how he and Alyssa are working this out, or are they frustrated and ready to jump on the slide to push Alyssa down?

It may be that Dave would reach a point at which his skill or willingness to continue the dialogue ends—the dialogue is a strategy for connection, after all, and connection is not the *only* need Dave wants to attend to. There's also consideration for the other children, safety, acceptance, and connection with the younger sibling. He might then decide to go up and physically remove Alyssa from the slide. But if he stays connected to his *motivation* for using physical strength, he would stay compassionate as he tries to meet, to the best of his ability, his needs for protection and cooperation, instead of acting with anger or an impulse to punish. Articulating *these* needs to Alyssa would make it much more likely that the whole interaction would end peacefully and in connection rather than alienation.

A Note on Timing

Most parent-child dialogues about ongoing conflicts take place in the middle of a struggle. While NVC can be very helpful in these high-intensity times, it is important to also find peaceful moments to talk about ongoing struggles. Though it can be hard to remember to talk *proactively*, conversations that start from connection rather than conflict can make a huge difference in both people's capacity to hear each other and work together to find strategies to meet both their needs.

If Dave is not satisfied with how the interaction with Alyssa ended, and if he experiences such interactions repeatedly, he might bring up his concerns *before* they go to the park next time. He might say, "When I think about going to the park I feel excited to play, but also worried that we might fight because I want to stay connected with you and enjoy our time together. Would you be willing to talk with me about what we might do to meet both our needs during our time at the park today?" Alyssa may be much more willing to hear his concerns now than she will be at the park, and she will be more likely to express her own feelings and needs openly. Together, over time, they will come up with creative strategies to prevent and address these conflicts.

Consider what your ongoing struggles revolve around, and make a time to talk about them that is likely to work for both you and your child. If your struggle is about bedtime, or brushing teeth, connect with your child in the morning or afternoon. If your struggle has to do with getting out of the house in the morning, talk about it in the evening. If your struggle is about watching TV, or playing video games, talk when you are out of the house, or enjoying each other's company over a snack—not when your child is in the middle of a favorite program and wants to watch just one more thing.

EXERCISE 3
Transforming Habitual Responses

1.　Imagine each of the following examples is something your child says to you. Write down how you might respond habitually. Then write your feelings and needs that give rise to this response. Then write down your guess of your child's feelings and needs that might lead them to say what they are saying. (You may want to use the feelings and needs lists found at the back of this booklet.)

　　a.　Your child says to you: "You're not the boss. You can't tell me what to do."

Habitual response: _____ .

Self empathy: I feel _____ because I need _____ .

Empathy Guess: Do you feel ___ because you need _____ ?

b. Your child says to you: "You're a bad mommy/daddy."

Habitual response: _____ .

Self empathy: I feel _____ because I need _____ .

Empathy Guess: Do you feel ___ because you need _____ ?

2.　Using your own, real-life example, write down something your child says to you that's hard for you to hear. Follow the same format of habitual response, then self-empathy and an empathy guess.

a. Your child says to you: _____ .

Habitual response: _____ .

Self empathy: I feel _____ because I need _____ .

Empathy Guess: Do you feel ___ because you need _____ ?

b. Your child says to you: _____ .

Habitual response: _____ .

Self empathy: I feel _____ because I need _____ .

Empathy Guess: Do you feel _____ because you need _____ ?

Compare your responses with some of the examples I've given in the previous sections.

EXERCISE 4
Timing Conversations

1. Think about an ongoing conflict you have with your child, and write down what the conflict is about.

2. What might be a good time to talk about this conflict?

3. What do you think your child's feelings and needs might be in relation to this situation?

4. Consider what you might say to your child. Write down a clear observation, feeling, need, and a request.

Consider: Is this request taking into account your child's needs? If not, think about at least two more requests that may help meet your needs and also include your understanding of your child's needs.

For an introduction to dealing with anger using NVC, see the booklet *What's Making You Angry?* available from The Center for Nonviolent Communication.

Hearing the "Yes" in the "No"

"NO!" The dreaded word has been spoken. You asked your child to do something reasonable, like put on sunscreen on a hot, sunny day. Wash her hands before a meal. Put her shoes on so you can get out of the house. Pick up the books and clothes she left scattered in the living room. Brush her teeth before going to bed. Go to bed.

Yet your child—at a year, two, three, four or fourteen—has a mind of her own. You love that mind of hers, her growing independence and assertiveness, her desire to decide what she wants to do and when. But you wish she would be reasonable!

You wish she would do, without so much fuss, what you want her to do.

Negotiating the gap between what we want and what our children want can strain our patience and skill level to their limit. Parenting books attest to this, as one after another focuses on how to get our children to do what we want them to do—whether through "effective discipline," rewards, punishments, or dialogue.

Consider a situation Shelly, mother of a three-year-old, wrote me about:

Sometimes Grace refuses to get into the car seat, in which case we "force" her in. This issue involves protecting my child from harm. It could be argued that we could simply choose to wait and not go anywhere in the car until we can talk her into getting in herself. However, like most people, we are always rushing around, and waiting is very rarely a practical option. What can we do?

An NVC Dialogue

An NVC dialogue may or may not help Shelly solve this problem quickly, but it will certainly support her in having the quality of relationship she wants with Grace. The key to fostering connection in the face of a "no" is to remember that "no" is always "yes" to something else and, as such, it is the *beginning*, not the end of a conversation. If Shelly chooses to take the time to connect with her daughter—which sometimes *does* move things more quickly—the dialogue might look something like this:

Shelly: Hey, it's time to leave to go to Grandpa's.

Grace: NO! NO! NO!

Shelly: Are you enjoying what you're doing and want to continue doing it? *(Instead of hearing the "no," Shelly listens for what Grace is saying "yes" to by guessing her feeling of pleasure and her needs for play and choice.)*

Grace: YES! I want to keep gardening!

Shelly: You're really having fun gardening?

Grace: Yes!

Shelly: I'm enjoying seeing how fun it is for you. I'm worried because I like getting to places when I say I will. *(Instead of coming back with her own "no," Shelly expresses her feelings and her need for responsibility.)* If we want to get to Grandpa's when I told him we'll be there, this is the time to leave. So would you be willing to get into the car seat now? *(Shelly ends with a request that lets Grace know what she can do to help Shelly meet her needs.)*

Grace: NO! I want to garden now!

Shelly: I'm confused about what to do. I like when you do things you enjoy, and I also want to do what I said I was going to do. *(Shelly shows Grace that she cares about meeting both their needs.)* Would you be willing to go into the car seat in 5 minutes so we could get there soon? *(Shelly offers a strategy that might meet both their needs, again in the form of a request.)*

Grace: Okay.

Or maybe it wasn't that easy . . .

Grace: NO!!! I don't want to go! I want to stay home!

Shelly: Are you VERY frustrated now? YOU want to choose what YOU are going to do? *(Shelly connects with Grace by showing her understanding and acceptance of Grace's intense emotions and her need for autonomy.)*

Grace: Yes! I want to garden!

Shelly: I see. I'm feeling sad because I want to make plans that work for everyone. Would you be willing to think with me about some ideas of what to do that would work for both of us right now? *(Again, Shelly expresses her care for meeting both their needs and comes up with a new strategy that might also meet Grace's needs for choice and autonomy.)*

Grace: Okay.

Depending on the child's age, ideas for strategies to meet everyone's needs might come from the parent with feedback from the child, or from both people. Children as young as two or three may surprise you by coming up with strategies to meet everyone's needs, sometimes innovative and workable ones the adults had not considered.

Even if Grace were still to say "no" at this stage, NVC continues to offer Shelly options for connection with herself and with her daughter. With repeated experiences that give a child confidence that adults respect her needs as well as their own, she will steadily develop greater capacity for considering others' needs and acting to meet them. Meanwhile, Shelly will discover that these moments are opportunities to strengthen her understanding of herself and of her core needs in relation to parenting, by acting with care both for herself and for her daughter.

Linking Strategies to Needs

In using NVC, we focus on how to meet all of our needs, sometimes postponing decisions until we have made a connection with each other that will be the basis for a solution. Having connected, Shelly and Grace might come up with a variety of strategies, depending on which needs are most alive for them. Shelly might realize that she could meet her need for responsibility by calling Grandpa and making the date an hour later. She might choose to meet her need for consideration by expressing her feelings and needs more passionately and seeking understanding from her daughter. Or she might connect with her needs for harmony and ease and choose to change the plans. If the plans are changed out of a clear choice to meet needs, this is quite different from "giving in" to the child's "whims."

Connecting with Grace's needs might yield other strategies. Grace might have a passionate need for play, which might be met by coming up with a plan for what she'll do when they get to Grandpa's. She might have a powerful need for autonomy, which might be met by leaving it up to her to decide when she's ready. She also has a need for contributing to others' lives. If Shelly finds a way to express her own feelings and needs and make clear requests of Grace, she might help her connect with her own intrinsic need to contribute to others so that it becomes *Grace's choice* to get into the car seat rather than a "power struggle" that she loses.

What Difference Does Hearing "Yes" Make?

When our children say "no" and we hear "no," we are left with two often unsatisfying options. Either we accommodate their "no" or we override it. When we choose to transform our children's "no" into an understanding of the "yes" behind it, we gain deeper insight into what motivates our children's actions: needs that are shared by all human beings. A deeper understanding of our children usually leads to both of us feeling more connected to each other. People who are connected have a greater capacity to think creatively about strategies to meet their needs, extend their goodwill toward one another, and exercise more patience and tolerance when their needs are not met in the moment. In my family, as in other families who practice NVC, this does *not* mean that we always solve everything easily. But it does mean that we regularly nurture our connection through these dialogues, and that we trust one another more and more deeply with our feelings and needs. This is the quality of relationship that I want for all parents and children.

Changing our responses to our children's "no" means, in part, letting go of the power we have over our children by relinquishing (or at least reducing) our own "no" to them. It means being willing to let go of our attachment to our strategies based on understanding our own and our children's deeper needs. It means focusing on the nature of the relationship we want to have with our children, what we want to teach them, and what kind of world we want to create with them.

Yet using NVC does not mean giving up on meeting *our* needs. Our deep human needs matter, and we have powerful tools with which to meet them: expressing our feelings and needs passionately, and learning to identify what might help meet our needs without an attending cost for our children. Without blaming, shaming, or demanding acquiescence, we can meet our needs by connecting with ourselves and our children.

There is a risk to making requests of our children instead of demands or ultimatums: they just might say "no," and we might think that we have to accept it. Of course, we haven't lost much, because children often say "no" even to our demands! How delightful, then, to discover that by hearing the "yes," we gain freedom to not take "no" for an answer. We can use a "no"—from our children, our partners, ourselves—as the beginning of a rich dialogue that can bring all of us closer and move us in the direction of meeting *all* of our needs.

EXERCISE 5
Working with "No"

Key Ideas:

- "No" can be the beginning of a conversation.

- We can continue the dialogue by connecting with what needs the other person is trying to meet by saying "no." Another way to think about this: What need is the person saying "yes" to when she or he says "no" to my request?

- We can reach a mutual "yes" through a commitment to meeting everyone's needs—not just ours, not just others'. When our children trust this commitment, they will be more open to considering our needs.

1. Write down something you've said to your child that you would like to say using NVC. Translate the statement into observations, feelings, needs, and requests. (You may want to use the feelings and needs lists found at the back of this booklet)

   Original statement: _____ .

   When I see/hear _____ .

   I feel _____ .

   Because I need _____ .

   Would you be willing to _____ ?

2. Now imagine your child says "no" to your request. What are your feelings and needs when you hear or think about the "no?" (Most of us have a hard time hearing no, so self-empathy may be helpful.)

I feel _____ .

Because I need _____ .

3. Think of the child who is saying the "no." What might be
    your child's feelings and needs? Or, what is your child
    saying "yes" to? What needs is she or he trying to meet?

    The child may feel: _____ .

    Because the child may need: _____ .

4. In writing or as a role play with your life partner, use NVC
    in the following dialogue format. Where it says "child,"
    imagine what your child might say in response and write
    it down:

    You: Do you feel ____ because your need for ____ is unmet?

    Child: _____ .

    You *(empathy)*: Do you feel ____ because you need _____ ?

    Child: _____ .

    You *(expression)*: I feel _____ because I need _____ .

    Would you be willing to _____ ?

    Child: _____ .

    You *(choose expression or empathy)*: _____ .

    Child: _____ .

    You *(choose expression or empathy)*: _____ .

Though the dialogue may not be complete, pause and consider
what you've learned from continuing it beyond the initial "no"
and beyond your initial reaction. How do you feel now? What
needs of yours were met by trying to connect with your child?

Protective Use of Force

Protective force is a complex concept in NVC because, when our needs are not met, the temptation always exists to justify using force as a protective measure. Yet there are times when protective force is needed. Kate wrote me about such a situation with her toddler:

> *Daniel has recently gotten into the habit of playfully kicking me while I'm changing his diaper. I am seven months pregnant and his kicks go right to my belly, and I'm concerned about my and my baby's safety. I've tried talking to him, but he doesn't respond. I was about to threaten him with, "If you kick again I'll have to let you have some quiet time in your room." Then I started reading about NVC, and now I'm not sure what to do. Isn't he too young to understand feelings and needs?*

Clearly, the issue here is one of safety. The first thing for Kate to do is to protect herself and her baby. In NVC we talk about using protective force when we want to protect someone's safety and there is no time, skill, or willingness to talk things over. The difference between protective and punitive force is that our intention, as much as possible, is to *protect* rather than to teach or to punish. Kate can try her best to prevent Daniel from kicking, not because she judges that it's *wrong* (because judgments tend to block one's ability to see the other person with compassion), but out of a desire to protect herself and to help him care for her and his sibling. As soon as everyone is safe, she can go back to the dialogue—that's when connecting (and learning) may happen.

I will address Kate's question about language in the next section.

EXERCISE 6
Considering Use of Force

Think of a situation with your child in which you are using physical force to achieve the result you want. *(By physical force I mean actions such as spanking, but also actions such as picking up a child and placing her in the car seat against her will.)*

1. What is the situation?

2. What's your rationale for using force?

3. What needs are you hoping to meet by using force? How do you feel when you recognize these needs?

4. What needs are you not meeting by using force? How do you feel when you recognize these needs?

5. Considering both sets of needs, can you imagine other strategies for meeting your needs?

NVC and Language

Because NVC appears to rely on verbal exchanges, it seems difficult—if not utterly impossible—to apply with young children. Yet at its heart, NVC is only peripherally about "language." Much more centrally, it is about a set of principles and approaches to connecting with ourselves and with others, such as the ideas of prioritizing connection, attending to everyone's needs, looking for the need behind whatever behavior we don't like, and sharing power instead of using power-over strategies.

In my experience, NVC practice with toddlers is often more about what I'm doing inside myself—how I'm talking with myself about what is going on with me and with my child—than about negotiation. Yet I also want to verbalize my understanding of what's going on for both of us, at least some of the time, even if I think my child doesn't understand the language, because it helps me connect with both of our feelings and needs. This, in turn, helps me calm down and find strategies that will more likely work for both of us. I also want to talk out loud because I believe this is how language and emotional literacy is acquired. If I don't express (and expand) my own feelings and needs vocabulary, my child will absorb only the words for the limited repertoire of feelings that we tend to disclose in our culture. It is my hope for children to be more emotionally aware than that.

When working out problems with small children, just as with anyone, I suggest to parents to focus on the *quality of connection* between them and their children. Paying attention to their own feelings and needs is a crucial step toward connecting.

Returning now to Kate's situation with her son, Kate may first check in with herself: Is she feeling scared because she wants the baby to be safe? Is she frustrated because she'd like cooperation in protecting herself and the baby? Is she sad because she wants Daniel to care about her well-being? Is she confused about how to connect with Daniel in this situation? She will be on track in expressing these feelings and needs to her son, *even if she thinks he may not understand her.* The only reason not to verbalize is if she suspects that the amount of words is more than Daniel wants to hear. In that case, she can remind herself that the verbal exchange is only a strategy and continue to focus on how to connect with fewer words or non-verbally.

In order to fully connect with Daniel, however, Kate will probably want to try to understand what might be going on for him as well. Why would he be kicking her in the stomach? She said he was doing so *playfully,* so it's possible that he may be excited and wanting to play. It's also possible that he may be feeling antsy during diaper changes, and that he wants more freedom of movement. Perhaps he is frustrated by lying down because he wants more of a sense of choice or power. Or maybe he is simply trying to connect with Kate and engage her attention.

Each of these guesses will lead Kate to a slightly different strategy for how to try to meet Daniel's needs, and meeting his needs is the surest way I know to protect herself and her baby while maintaining connection with Daniel. Perhaps playing with him for a few minutes before diaper changes would help meet his need for play? Perhaps making a "diaper changing game" that he enjoys—funny faces, jokes, singing, trying to catch his toes to kiss them—would help him trust that the two of them are engaged and connected? Perhaps changing diapers while standing, or finding a way for him to choose when to have his diaper changed, would meet his need for more choice and power? (One parent shared with me that when she started asking her toddler to tell her when she was willing to have her diaper changed, months of diaper change conflicts came to an end.)

When young children behave in ways parents don't understand and don't like, parents can give them a great gift: they can tune into what their children's hearts are saying, and try their best to respond from their own hearts. When parents and children are heart-connected, a diaper change is no longer a chore to get through without getting hurt, but an opportunity—the same opportunity that exists in every moment in life—to be present with oneself and another human being and to grow in trust and joy.

EXERCISE 7
Beyond Language

In the following scenarios, guess what might be the baby or child's feelings and needs, and the parent's feelings and needs, and then write down at least two strategies for meeting both people's needs that don't rely on using verbal NVC (you can also explore the same scenarios using verbal NVC). Keep in mind that the strategies don't have to solve the problem. Recognize the specific issue at hand, but focus on the quality of connection between the individuals involved, now or in the future. (You may want to use the feelings and needs lists found at the back of this booklet.)

1. Sitting at her high chair, a one-year-old throws food on the floor. When her father asks her to stop, she smiles and throws down more food.

   Baby's feelings might be: _____ .

   Baby's needs might be: _____ .

   Father's feelings and needs might be: _____ .

   Possible strategies for moving toward connection might be:

   _____ .

2. A three-year-old says he won't brush his teeth. When his mother says brushing teeth is really important, and she won't read him a book until he brushes his teeth, he puts his hands on his ears and says, "I'm not listening!"

   Son's feelings might be: _____ .

   Son's needs might be: _____ .

   Mother's feelings and needs might be: _____ .

Possible strategies for moving toward connection might be:

_____ .

3. It's 7:00 p.m. and a 10-year-old has not done her homework. The mother reminds her daughter about the homework, but the daughter walks to the living room and turns on the television.

Daughter's feelings might be: _____ .

Daughter's needs might be: _____ .

Mother's feelings and needs might be: _____ .

Possible strategies for moving toward connection might be:

_____ .

4. A 16-year-old comes home an hour after the time he had agreed to. His father says, "When you're not home at the time that we agreed, I feel so anxious because I want you to be safe. I'm also angry because I want to trust that my needs would matter to you. Would you tell me where you were?" The son says, "With friends," goes into his room and shuts the door.

Son's feelings might be: _____ .

Son's needs might be: _____ .

Father's feelings and needs might be: _____ .

Possible strategies for moving toward connection might be:

_____ .

Mediating Between Children

Young children invariably go through periods when it seems that their purpose in life is to take anything that another child within their view is playing with. Witnessing delightful cooperative or parallel play turn into a tug-of-war, with both children likely to end up in tears, often reduces the adults to a bundle of nerves right along with the children.

Before we make sense of how to intervene, let's try to understand our own intense reactions to these situations. Whether our child is grabbing or losing the toy, many of us are familiar with the immediate, visceral reaction of anger, of wanting to "right" the "wrong" we just witnessed. The anger we feel is understandable. We want to protect our children from emotional and physical pain. We worry that if our children cannot manage themselves in ways that are socially acceptable, they will suffer. We have strong values about kindness, sharing, cooperation, and justice, and we want to teach those to our children. We long to contribute to our children's ability to live with others in peace.

When a "grabbing incident" takes place, however, we don't usually stop to think about our values and wishes for our children. While some of us let the children work things out for themselves, most of us intervene to determine who had the object first and to make sure it is returned to that child; to remind or enforce a general rule about sharing or taking turns; or to administer a consequence such as a "time out." Yet while these interventions may provide momentary relief, I believe they undermine our ability to meet our own and our children's deeper needs.

So how can we use conflicts between children as an opportunity for all of us to learn to live in peace, to meet all our needs, and to internalize kindness, cooperation, and compassion? NVC offers a way to do that. I'd like to illustrate with an experience I had a couple of years ago.

NVC with Two Toddlers

Eighteen-month-old Jacob and his dad were visiting three-year-old Noah and his mom. When it came time to leave, Jacob clearly had every intention of leaving with Noah's little car. Noah was sometimes agreeable to other children borrowing his things, but this happened to be his only little car. When I checked with him to see if he was willing for Jacob to borrow it, his whole body went into "grabbing mode"—his muscles tensed, his eyes focused on Jacob's hand, and he seemed ready to jump on Jacob to repossess the car. Noticing the imminent grab, I asked Noah to hold on so we could try to talk with Jacob about it, and since he is used to resolving conflicts with NVC, he relaxed. If he had not relaxed, I would have begun the dialogue with my attention on him.

I tried to reflect to Jacob my guess about his feelings and needs. "You like this car? You want to be able to keep playing with it?" Jacob looked at me intently and held on tight to the car. I told him, "You know, this is Noah's only little car and he wants to have it in the house. Would you be willing to give it back to him?" Jacob's body language indicated a clear "no."

Noah tensed once again, and Jacob's dad said to me, "It's OK, we'll just take it out of his hand." I asked them both to wait and give our conversation a chance. I stayed focused on Jacob. "You really like things with wheels? You want something with wheels?" I looked around for a strategy that would meet Jacob's need for choice of the kind of toy he plays with, and found one, so I asked, "Would you like this Lego™ train with wheels?" (Based on prior experience, I was pretty confident that Noah wouldn't have an objection to Jacob taking the Lego train.) Jacob happily took the Lego with wheels while continuing to hold on to the little car. Now he had two of Noah's toys!

At that moment, I did not have any evidence that what I was doing was "working." So why would I keep going? Because I believe that all people have an innate desire to contribute to others' well being. Even when children are very young and absorbed in meeting their own needs, one of their needs is to contribute to others. I believe we can tap their generosity by exhibiting trust in their need to contribute, by articulating it and inviting them to act on it *without any coercion*. The lack of coercion is crucial because generosity does not arise when we are forced into it.

Model What You Want to See

Equally important to me is modeling for children that all people's needs matter and can be met. Using NVC, I do this by actively showing that *their* needs matter to me. The key here is modeling for children the behavior we want to teach them. If we don't want them to grab, we don't grab. Almost every time I am around a group of children, I see an adult say "no grabbing" while taking a toy from the hands of a resisting child and giving it to another.

This action may seem logical in our adult eyes because we are acting to meet our needs for justice, consideration, and supporting children. However, it is not inherently different from the action of a child who grabs a toy because she wants to meet her needs for play, autonomy, and exploration.

When Jacob still did not give the car back after I gave him the train, his dad and Noah tensed once again, though Jacob seemed quite absorbed in our conversation. Jacob's dad repeated his suggestion of taking the car back. I spoke to them while keeping eye contact with Jacob. "I would like to keep talking with Jacob. I don't want to force him to give up the car. I'd like to keep talking and see if he would be *willing* to give back the car." Noah then moved toward Jacob, while Jacob's dad and I watched, and spoke to him directly. "Jacob," he said, "why don't you take the Lego train? You can take it home, and give me back the car." When Jacob did not immediately give back the car, Noah reached his hand to take it from him once again, but I moved closer and expressed again, to both of them, how much I wanted to talk until we figured this out. At that moment, Jacob turned to Noah, fully relaxed, and handed him the little car. It seemed to me that Jacob needed to trust that he was not going to be physically *forced* to do something he did not want to do, in order for him to act on his *own will* to consider another's wishes. His dad seemed awe-struck by his behavior.

But I was not surprised. An inner shift almost always happens for at least one of the people involved in a conflict when NVC is used—and often for both. When we trust that our own needs really matter to others, we can often relax about the particular strategies we are choosing at that moment. If Jacob had not shifted, I would have turned to Noah to see if he would shift. Sometimes, just the act of checking in with both children meets their need for trust that my request is not a demand, and that both their needs matter. This contributes to their willingness to consider the other.

Attending to Everyone's Needs

If I want to use NVC, then I turn my attention to identifying and acknowledging everyone's needs. Both children who wanted the car had a need for autonomy—to choose what to do. We all have that need, and it comes up most fiercely when we are told that we "have to" do something. Hearing that the car might be taken from him, Jacob held on to it ever more tightly. To meet his need for autonomy, he had to find a way to experience giving back the car as *his* choice. Noah, on the other hand, also needed choice about what happens with his things. It would be hard for him to agree to have other children play with his toys if he thought that meant he would lose choice about where the toys ended up.

I wanted to nurture autonomy—*and* consideration—in both children. Had I grabbed the car from Jacob, I would have sent him *and* Noah a message about the necessity of using force, even while I told them both not to. So I held myself back and took a leap of faith: that we could work this out without force; that at least one child will choose to act out of consideration of the other; and that in this process we will have acted not only to resolve this one conflict peacefully, but also to nurture in both children trust in the possibility of care, understanding, and peace.

Here is my hope for all children, and for human beings: that we may nurture in ourselves and in our children faith in the possibility of peace—and the capacities to make peace happen. We can contribute to this by intervening in ways that model what we want our children to learn.

EXERCISE 8
Mediating Between Children

Think of a conflict situation between your children where you have not been satisfied with your mediation. (If you have a single child, think of a situation with friends.)

1. Briefly describe the situation in observation language.

2. How do you feel in relation to this situation?

3. What needs do you have in relation to this situation?

4. What request do you have of yourself or your children in relation to this situation?

5. Think about one child, and write down your understanding

of that child's feelings and needs. Write it down as an empathy guess.

6. Think of the second child, and write down your understanding of that child's feelings and needs. Write it down as an empathy guess.

7. In writing or in practice with a partner express your own feelings, needs and requests, and respond with empathy to each child's expression. Remember to guess the children's feelings and needs rather than simply reflecting what you heard them say.

Praise

I believe that helping, supporting, or contributing in any way to another person is one of the sweetest experiences in life, and receiving such contributions is glorious, too. So I end every workshop I lead with at least a short segment on using NVC to express gratitude and appreciation. I also make sure to explore this topic because I believe it's important to reduce our dependence on praise and rewards.

Consider this question Mark, a father of two school-aged children, asked me:

> I have always tried to encourage my children in their development through praise of certain behaviors, though I don't believe in praise or criticism of the person. For instance: "I notice you are doing a great job being patient, or generous, etc." Or: "Thank you for being so cooperative and respectful during violin practice. Great work!" What's your perspective on praise?

I feel worried about using praise, even when it focuses on an action rather than on an individual. I avoid praise for the same reasons I avoid criticism; indeed, I see them as surprisingly similar. Whether I praise or criticize someone's action, I imply that I am their evaluator, that I am engaged in rating their work or what they have done.

Here's a brief example. One afternoon, my family and some friends were throwing a Frisbee™ outside. When my son, who was three at the time, threw the Frisbee, it flew in a long arc and landed across the courtyard. The adult friend who was with us exclaimed, "You're a great Frisbee thrower!" My son picked up the Frisbee, threw it again, and it flopped just a couple of feet from him. He said, "I'm a bad Frisbee thrower." It seemed to me that he got very clearly the message that one was either a good thrower or a bad one.

Moving from Judgments to Observations

Indeed, when we praise, we are implying that the "good" can turn "bad." But why put ourselves in the position of evaluator at all? We can express our active engagement with our children's actions or creations without evaluating them. Instead of using good and bad, we can try to make observations and to connect with whether certain behaviors do or do not meet our needs. "Good Frisbee thrower" might turn into expressing a simple observation: "That Frisbee flew across the entire courtyard." It might also include expressing feelings and needs, in simplified language: "Wow, I like watching it glide in the air." Then, when the Frisbee falls flat, it's not a bad throw. Perhaps it's something like this: "That one fell close to you." And then, based on whether this seems important to the child, an empathic guess might be added: "Are you disappointed? You want to be able to throw farther?" Or, "Are you enjoying practicing so you can throw it as far as you want?"

I have another, more serious concern about praise. Praise and rewards create a system of extrinsic motivations for behavior. Children (and adults) end up taking action in order to receive the praise or rewards. I want to support children's intrinsic motivation to act—their pleasure in taking a particular action for its own sake, because they are connected to the needs they want to meet. I don't want anyone to throw a Frisbee, clean the house, do homework, or help a person in need, in order to be praised or accepted. I'd like people to do these things out of the joy of play or a desire to contribute to themselves and to others. This deep sense of pleasure is lost when the rewards are extrinsic. (I recommend Alfie Kohn's book, *Punished by Rewards,* to those who want to read more about this subject.)

Instead of praising or rewarding, NVC offers a powerful way to connect with people when we enjoy their actions: to express to them what they have done that has enriched our lives, our feelings about it, and what needs of ours were met. Let's take Mark's example above. He said to his child, "I notice you are doing a great job being patient." If he wants to use NVC, Mark would look for a clear observation, because "being patient" is an interpretation. He might say, "I noticed you occupied yourself the whole time I was on the phone without talking to me. I'm very grateful because I needed support to focus on the conversation." (The tone of voice and eye contact, of course, would communicate more of the warmth of the feeling than the words can convey.)

Mark's second example was this: "Thank you for being so cooperative and respectful during violin practice. Great work!" Again I would suggest first to focus on the observation. What did the child say or do that Mark interprets as cooperative or respectful? Then expand the expression to include feelings and needs. For example: "When you practiced your violin today for twenty minutes without a reminder from me, I felt so happy because I appreciate cooperation and peace between us. I was also excited because I love sharing music with you."

Like anything else in using NVC, the precise language is not so important. What matters is the intention to express our appreciation or gratitude not in order to motivate or evaluate, but as a way to connect and celebrate together. If we sometimes spontaneously call out, "Good job," let's not worry about it. But let's continue to explore taking ourselves out of the role of evaluator or motivator, and think more about reflecting what we see and speaking in the first person about the way it affects us, thereby giving our children the gift of acknowledgement and the sweetness of knowing that their actions have been a contribution.

EXERCISE 9
Gratitude and Appreciation

Key Ideas:

- Judging things as "good" or "right" is not different in essence from judging them as "bad" or "wrong"—they belong to the same paradigm, and our evaluation can easily shift from "good" to "bad." Translating our positive evaluations into NVC frees us from this paradigm and from the role of "judge."

* When we enjoy something or are grateful, expressing what needs of ours have been met can be powerful and deeply satisfying to our children and to us.

* By expressing our observations, feelings, and needs instead of praising, we contribute to meeting our children's needs for intrinsic motivation and for contribution.

1. Think of something your child has done which has affected your life in a way that you feel grateful for, or think of something your child has done that you have praised or might praise them for. Express your gratitude or "praise" in NVC:

What did your child do _____ ?

How do you feel in relation to what he or she did _____ ?

What needs of yours were met by this action _____ ?

2. Use the same process to identify something for which you are grateful to yourself as a parent:

What did I do or what am I doing _____ ?

How do I feel about what I did or what I am doing _____ ?

What needs of mine were or are met by this action _____ ?

Starting Out with NVC

Many parents who begin learning NVC experience a surge of hope and inspiration about what life in their family can be like. Yet sometimes, when they try to apply their new skills, they feel discouraged. As in every facet of life, it usually takes time to make a change. Focusing on feelings and needs and on making requests instead of demands can seem daunting at first. Yet NVC, like any new language, can be learned and incorporated into everyday life. Starting NVC when children are infants gives parents a wonderful head start by allowing them time to learn and practice self-empathy and to focus on recognizing needs and building trust and connection, but NVC can be introduced at *any* age, and family dynamics *can* be transformed.

Sometimes introducing NVC makes an immediate difference, as in Sharon's case. Right before lunch at a parents' workshop, Sharon, a single mother of two teens, asked to talk about what was awaiting her at home, where she was going to have lunch and then give her 15-year-old son a ride on her way back to the workshop. The night before, she had asked him to do a couple of chores before lunchtime. Yet she was quite sure that, when she got home, he would still be in bed. She anticipated with dread how the hour would unfold. She would reproach and demand, they would have a fight about the chores, and he wouldn't do them. She wondered how she might use NVC to handle this situation.

When a parent asks for help, it is tempting to offer advice or strategies. Yet in working with NVC, we try instead to offer the gift of our presence and to connect with the person, trusting that empathy is usually more needed than advice. So I offered Sharon empathy—the opportunity to connect more deeply with her feelings and needs in relation to this situation. What we connected with ranged from feelings of exhaustion and weariness because her needs for support and ease were not met, to feelings of discouragement and even despair because she needed more trust and connection with her son. Sharon cried as she related her deep sadness over the state of her relationship with both her teens. Before we broke for lunch, we reminded Sharon to express herself using the steps of NVC, and to empathize with her son's feelings and needs if he said "no" to her requests.

After lunch, all of us wanted to know what had happened at home. "You won't believe this," Sharon told us. She shared that when she got home, her son was indeed still sleeping. She woke him up and expressed her observations, feelings, needs, and a request for him to do the chores. Her son agreed, and did the first chore. A bit later, when she saw him sitting on the couch reading, she expressed herself again using the four steps of NVC, ending with a request for him to do the second chore. Her son agreed again. Then he turned to her and said, "Mom, why are you talking to me this way?" She replied, "Well, you know, I'm in a communication workshop this weekend." He said, "Keep it up, Mom. It's working."

Like Sharon, parents frequently report that changing the way they speak to their children can make a dramatic difference in how their children respond. One mother shared that the first time she used NVC when her children quarreled with each other was also the first time that she felt truly happy with the results of her mediation. Others have used the term "miraculous" to describe the change. When changes happen quickly, parents may feel encouraged to continue on this new path.

Other parents find that it may take considerable time and effort to shift deeply ingrained habits of communication and patterns of behavior. When changes are slow to come, parents often feel discouraged, confused, and overwhelmed. Parenting is immensely challenging under almost any circumstances. Trying to make a significant change in parenting styles can seem daunting. In such situations, it is crucial for parents to receive extra support, hopefully in the form of empathy, companionship, and learning with and from other adults. Networks of NVC practitioners are growing around the world, offering opportunities for such support. When NVC support is not available locally, resources may be available by phone or email (check the resources on the CNVC web site). And every person learning NVC can choose to create his or her own NVC group with friends or family members, in homes, schools, religious institutions, neighborhoods, or even work places.

Even when changes in patterns of relating are slow to come, parents comment on *internal* changes they experience. Personal healing, deeper self-connection, growing understanding of themselves and of their children, and increasing hope are among the gifts parents experience even when their own or their children's behavior is slow to change.

Recognizing Differences Among Children: Temperament and Development

As powerful and effective as it can be for addressing problems in the social and political arenas, the language of NVC *by itself* does not remedy the enormous challenges parents face when they don't have the financial or social resources to meet their own or their children's needs. NVC does not eliminate social inequities that relate to race, gender, class, sexual orientation, physical ability, and the like. And it does not prepare us for the particular challenges we face as parents in relation to the developmental, physical, and temperamental needs and phases of our individual children. Addressing the first two concerns is beyond the scope of this booklet, but I would like to highlight a few points in relation to development and temperament.

People of different ages and temperaments tend to experience certain needs particularly acutely. Understanding the key needs a certain child of a certain age may be experiencing can be very helpful for developing understanding and patience for the child, and for working with the challenges associated with meeting that child's key needs.

For example, one of the most powerful needs crawling babies and young toddlers typically experience is for physical exploration of their world. While all human beings share this need, children at this age are *compelled* to try to meet this need, even at a cost to meeting other needs (such as safety, or harmony in the household). They "have to" open cabinets, throw food, pull electrical cords and the like, because those actions are powerful strategies for meeting their need for exploration. When parents try to get toddlers to stop doing certain things, they are unlikely to succeed, and if they do succeed, it is at a cost to helping their children meet this crucial need.

One of the challenges of parenting is to employ as much creativity and energy as possible in an attempt to meet children's core needs in ways that the parents can support. In the example here, effectively baby-proofing one's home can go a long way toward relieving the stresses that arise when a crawler or toddler's need to explore is at its height.

Children also typically have a strong need for play. Play is a crucial strategy for children because it helps them meet their needs for learning, companionship, joy, exploration, discovery, power, creativity, and growth, among others. Because many adults do not make time for play, or do not experience an affinity for the kind of creative, imaginative play children engage in, they tend to miss opportunities to use play as a strategy for meeting everyone's needs. Many a power struggle could end in moments if the parent recognized the opening for playful interaction.

I recently watched a mother help her four-year-old transition from playing with a beloved friend who he and his family were visiting for the weekend to going back to his own home. When the mother first told him she wanted to leave soon, he said, "OK." She told him when five minutes were left, and he didn't respond. Then when she wanted to get into the car, he said no. The mother empathized with how happy he was to be with his friend and with his wish to extend their visit. She expressed her desire to leave given the long drive they had ahead of them. And then she said, "Here's a ticket to park your scooter. It's for parking space D-3." The boy took the ticket and purposefully rode his friend's scooter to "D-3." Then his mother said, "Now I'd like to see your plane ticket so you can board the plane." He showed her an imaginary ticket, she checked it for a moment, returned it, and told him his is the middle seat in the back. He got into the car happily.

"Parking space D-3" and the plane ticket were inventions as effective as they were compassionate. They were effective in the sense that they produced the result the mother was hoping for—ease and connection—while moving forward with the transition. But they were also compassionate, because they included and addressed the boy's needs as well: for care about his needs, for attention, for play, and, like his mother, for ease and connection as they moved forward in their lives together.

In the same way that a basic understanding of developmental needs can be helpful to some parents, a basic understanding of temperament differences can offer enormous relief to others. Our society tends to treat parenting as a generic experience, masking the significantly different challenges that parents of different children face. Babies are born different from each other, each with his or her own unique expression of human nature. While they share fundamental human needs, they experience and express these needs differently and in different intensities. Therefore, parenting different children can be a very different experience, and using NVC with different children will likewise be different.

One baby may tend to be more quiet and observant, enjoying

lying on a blanket while the parent attends to other things. Another baby may cry inconsolably as soon as she or he is not held. One child may thrive on connecting in the midst of conflict, while another will need lots of space when emotions run high. Many parents of children whose needs appear to be more intense feel profoundly overwhelmed, exhausted, discouraged, confused, or angry. It is easy in these situations for parents to judge themselves—or their children—harshly. Their own needs—for support, understanding, acceptance, peace of mind, hope, and others—are sorely under-met. I would like to contribute to these parents by expressly acknowledging the particular challenges they are facing, and by encouraging all parents to increase the resources they call upon outside their families by building community with others.

EXERCISE 10
Next Steps

1. When you consider parenting with NVC in the future:

    a. What needs are you hoping to meet? How do you feel when you consider these needs may be met?

    b. What needs are you concerned you may not meet? How do you feel when you consider these needs may not be met?

    c. Are there any strategies you can think of that would contribute to meeting these needs you're concerned about while still parenting with NVC?

2. What specifically might get challenging for you in living NVC with your family? (Include observations.)

3. If the challenge involves yourself, can you identify what your feelings and needs might be in this situation?

4. If the challenge involves another person, can you identify what that person's feelings and needs might be in this situation?

5. Is there specific help you would like to meet your need for

support in living NVC with your family, and if so, from whom? Can you identify specific observations, feelings, needs, and requests you might express to that person?

6. Is there anything else you want to write down to help you meet your needs?

Parenting for Peace

Open the newspaper and you will invariably find descriptions of a world far different from what we wish for our children. Locally and globally, we live with war, violence, and environmental destruction. What resources and skills do we need, as a society, to support peace and live in harmony with nature? How can parents contribute to society's transition to nonviolence? What can we teach our children that will really make the world different for their generation?

Some time ago my son, nearly four years old at the time, asked me to read a book about castles that he had picked up at the library. He picked the book because he loved the *Eyewitness* series and was methodically going through as many of those books as we could find, irrespective of their subject matter. But I didn't like this one. It depicted not only castles but also knights, armor, and weapons of all kinds used in battles in centuries past.

I was not ready for weapons. One of the things I enjoyed about my son not going to preschool and not watching TV was that his exposure to violence had been extremely limited. At that time, he had never said the word "gun" or played pretend violent games. He didn't know about war and people purposely hurting one another. But here was the castle book, and he wanted to read it.

I was not trying to shield my son from the reality of violence and suffering in the world—but I am often in a (privileged) position to choose how and when these realities enter our lives. I read him some of the book, adding numerous editorial comments. But when he asked to read the book again a few days later, I found myself saying that I'd rather not. When he asked why, I told him that I feel a lot of sadness about people being violent with one another because I believe human beings can find peaceful ways to solve their conflicts.

Questions, of course, ensued. In response to one of his questions, I shared with him that my sadness was related not only to the past, when there were knights and castles, but to the present as well: that people in the area where I grew up, Israelis and Palestinians, are also fighting. "Why are they fighting?" he asked. "Because they both want the same piece of land and they haven't figured out how to talk about it," I replied. "I'll teach them!" he volunteered. "What will you teach them?" I asked. "I'll teach them that they can each have some of the land, they can share," he replied easily. "The only problem," he continued, "is that I don't know how to find them."

I felt a mixture of joy and grief at his words. How wondrous to hear from my son—and from so many children—a desire to contribute to the world and a trust in the possibility of solving conflicts peacefully. Yet how apt his words were: "I don't know where to find them." How *do* we find the hearts of "enemies" so we can reach them with a message of peace? How do we find our *own* hearts and open them to those whose actions we object to profoundly?

This search for our own and others' hearts is at the core of my hope for peace, and has been the greatest influence on my parenting. My experience of parenting and teaching NVC convinces me that what happens in our families both mirrors and contributes to what happens in our societies. Just as "enemies" fail to see each other's humanity, so we, too, at times fail to relate with others—even loved ones—with compassion. The primary challenge most parents tell me about is that though they yearn for peace and harmony at home, they find themselves getting angry with their children more often and more quickly than they would like.

I would like parents to have more resources to address the root causes of anger, as well as to resolve conflicts and solve daily challenges. Unfortunately, the problem-solving models most of us follow rely on judgments, demands, consequences, and rewards. All these may seem effective at times, but they tend to reinforce the cycle of anger instead of abating it.

What children learn from such models is rarely what parents intend. Instead of learning about cooperation, harmony, and mutual respect, they are more likely to learn the hard lesson of domination: that whoever has more power gets to have his or her way, and that those who have less power can only submit or rebel. And so we continue the cycle of domination that is leading human beings ever closer to self-destruction.

As parents, we have a remarkable opportunity to live and model a different paradigm with our children, one that empowers them with life skills for connecting with others, resolving conflicts, and contributing to peace. Changing our conception of human nature is one key to developing these skills. NVC teaches that all human beings have the same deep needs, and that people can connect with one another when they understand and empathize with each other's needs. Our conflicts arise not because we have different needs but because we have different strategies for how to meet them. It is on the strategy level that we argue, fight, or go to war, especially when we deem someone else's strategy a block to our own ability to meet our needs.

Yet NVC suggests that behind *every* strategy, however ineffective, tragic, violent, or abhorrent to us, is an attempt to meet a need. This notion turns on its head the dichotomy of "good guys" and "bad guys" and focuses our attention on the human being behind every action. When we understand the needs that motivate our own and others' behavior, we have no enemies. We can see the humanity in every person, even if we find his or her behavior deeply disturbing. With our tremendous resources and creativity, we can and—I hope—we *will* find new strategies for meeting all our needs.

Transforming parenting is hugely challenging in the context of the daily, overwhelming reality of family life. Yet this transformation enables a profound depth of connection and trust among family members. And beyond its impact on individual families, deeply connected parenting can lead our society's movement toward a world where everyone's needs matter, and peace is a reality—perhaps for our children's generation, perhaps for future generations. This will happen when human beings learn to speak the language of compassion.

About Inbal Kashtan

Inbal Kashtan is the Parenting Project coordinator for the Center for Nonviolent Communication. She also facilitates public workshops and retreats, leads trainings in organizations, coleads an NVC leadership development program, and creates curricula for learning NVC. Inbal lives with her family in Oakland, California, USA. You may contact Inbal at inbal@cnvc.org, or find information on joining the NVC-parenting email group at www.cnvc.org.

LEARN MORE about NVC and parenting at www.NonviolentCommunication.com
Sign up for our monthly NVC Quick Connect e-Newsletter, find expert articles, and more!

The Center for Nonviolent Communication
Find local, national and international training opportunities, trainer certification info, and a variety of other NVC educational materials at: **www.CNVC.org**

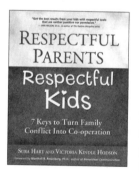

Respectful Parents, Respectful Kids
7 Keys to Turn Family Conflict Into Co-operation
by Sura Hart and Victoria Kindle Hodson

$17.95 – Trade Paper 7.5x9.25, 256pp
ISBN: 978-1-892005-22-9

Stop the Struggle—Find the Co-operation and Mutual Respect You Want!

Do more than simply correct bad behavior—finally unlock your parenting potential. Use this handbook to move beyond typical discipline techniques and begin creating an environment based on mutual respect, emotional safety, and positive, open communication. *Respectful Parents, Respectful Kids* offers *7 Simple Keys* to discover the mutual respect and nurturing relationships you've been looking for.

Use these 7 Keys to:

- Set firm limits without using demands or coercion
- Achieve mutual respect without being submissive
- Successfully prevent, reduce, and resolve conflicts
- Empower your kids to open up, co-operate, and realize their full potential
- Make your home a **No-Fault Zone** where trust thrives

Available from PuddleDancer Press, the Center for Nonviolent Communication, all major bookstores, and Amazon.com. Distributed by Independent Publisher's Group: 800-888-4741.

SAVE 10% at NonviolentCommunication.com with coupon code: **bookads**